Contents

	Contributor	Page
Foreword	Robert Smedley	5
Introduction	Ray Dwerryhouse	7
I teach...	Bernard Sheridan	9
I teach...	Sabeen Hussain	12
I teach...	Fritha Watson	15
I teach...	Matthew Mugan	19
I teach...	Carmel Gibbons	23
I teach...	Craig Gelling	26
I teach...	Davinder Johal	30
I teach...	Benjamin Smith	33
I teach...	Anonymous	36
The Lecturer's Lot	Peter Kirwin	38
I teach...	Andrew Morris	41
I teach...	Norma Kelly	44
I teach...	Saqib Hussain	47
I teach...	Catherine Shiel	50
I teach...	Peter Raftery	54
I teach...	Danielle Vipond	56
I teach...	Lorraine Compton	58
A Note on Reflection	Catherine Shiel & Amy Johnson	61
Reaching Out to Communities	Vicky Duckworth	63
How to Apply for Teacher Training	Jacqui Howe	67
Useful Websites		69
Routes into Teaching		70
Afterword	Editorial Team	72

Special Thanks

The editorial team would like to thank Gina Eastwood for her help with the initial development of this book.

Foreword

It is with great pleasure that I write the foreword for this book of journeys into teaching, all of which have been shared for the first time. Although the people in the stories have followed a wide variety of paths before entering teaching, it is the road into teaching that binds them today and in the future.

As you read the accounts in this book, you will see how the writers have overcome their fears, stepped out of their comfort zone and taken up the challenge to teach.

This book came about as a result of many discussions between many trainee teachers involving their life experience and their route into teaching. I hope you will be able to see the open and transparent way in which the students have compiled their stories for others to learn from and be inspired by.

I invite you to read and enjoy this book and finally to consider what you can bring to the lives of others as you contemplate entering this noble profession.

We are proud that the Faculty of Education at Edge Hill University has linked with the Helena Kennedy Foundation, a registered charity established to encourage social inclusion and widening participation in further and higher education by awarding bursaries to deserving students. All royalties from the book will go into this fund.

I do hope you are inspired, as I have been, by the stories of strength, courage and integrity and I wish you all the best in the path you choose to follow.

Robert Smedley, Dean
Faculty of Education, Edge Hill University

I teach... because it is the power of teaching that enables you to empower others.

Robert Smedley, Dean
Faculty of Education, Edge Hill University

Introduction

We are in the midst of a period of rapid change. Economic crisis, climate and structural change, and demographic developments, including ageing and migration, all pose huge challenges. Young people face working lives which demand great flexibility, frequent shifts between employers and roles, and a very high degree of adaptability. Indeed, the jobs which some existing 11 year olds will get have perhaps not even been invented or thought about yet.

To meet these demands, the education system needs the capacity for innovation and creativity. All providers of education from Primary through to the Post-Compulsory sector need to maximise the effective use of resources, and create and apply knowledge in new ways. Leaders in education also have to recognise that innovation partly depends on being able to leave behind established assumptions.

Good teachers are inspirational. The impact of a good teacher is something that has affected most of us at some time in our lives. A good teacher is a role model for their students and can communicate their experiences of life and give students a new outlook. Good teachers are not stereotypical. They come from a variety of backgrounds and experiences. They provide role models for students who are marginalised, for those who have learning and physical disabilities, and for those who have been socially excluded.

It is vital that the teaching profession attracts a wide range of motivated, creative and innovative individuals who have that important human element which enables them to pull it all together in the classroom.

The stories in this book serve to indicate the variety of people who enter the teaching profession, why they have done so, what barriers they have overcome, what they can offer as teachers, and finally what rewards that teaching brings them. It will, I am certain, motivate and inspire those thinking of teaching as a career.

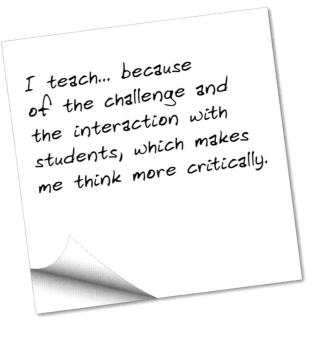

I teach... because of the challenge and the interaction with students, which makes me think more critically.

Ray Dwerryhouse
Assistant Head of Post-Compulsory Education and Training
Faculty of Education, Edge Hill University

Name: Bernard Sheridan
Age: 50
Qualifications: BA (Hons) American Studies/IT, BA Youth Justice, MA Criminal Justice, 3rd year Doctorate student
Subjects Taught: Criminal Justice, Criminology
Interesting Fact: I trace family history and teach others how to do this.

I teach... because, through my school and young adult life, I was told I was stupid. I don't want others to miss out on opportunities because they are being told the same.

What a roller coaster ride into education! At times I've felt like the scarecrow making his way to the Emerald City, in the hope that the Great Oz would give him a brain.

In my mind I 'failed' the 11+, 'failed' to pass all my secondary school exams and 'failed' to realise my mother's dream of my becoming a doctor. I grew up believing that I was stupid and that only clever people went to university.

I left secondary school at 16 with a few CSEs and a father who allowed me just one year at college before having to find employment to help my parents support our reasonably sized family (I'm the eldest of 6 children).

So at 17, off I went into the world of work, always dreaming but never expecting. At 20 I joined the police service and, although I loved my job, I always felt inferior to graduate officers.

As time passed I determined that one day, even if it's when I retire, I could perhaps go to university, get a degree and then start to believe I could be clever.

In 1999, however, things changed. I was seconded for a year to The Prince's Trust as a team leader where, by chance, I was asked to help out in a local youth club and where, by coincidence, Liverpool Hope University College were advertising its ReachOut programme providing teaching in the community which, after six years part-time study, could lead to a degree. I jumped at the chance resulting in a BA (Hons), a 2:1 at that!

I was subsequently seconded to a Youth Offending Team working alongside social workers, probation officers, education and health agency workers. To help in the role, I decided to jump straight back into education. I completed an MA in Criminal Justice with Liverpool Hope University, graduating in July 2007, and just to push the boundary a little more, I completed a further undergraduate degree with Nottingham Trent University in Youth Justice at the same time as I was studying for my MA.

My involvement with a university, mixing with students both full and part-time, the encouragement and commitment of tutors, the support provided by the library and IT departments, as well as a host of others, would have me recommend students to a university without reserve.

Have I finished with further education? I don't think so just yet. I applied to complete a Professional Doctorate in Criminal Justice with the University of Portsmouth in 2007 and was accepted onto this course. I'm now in the third year of this programme but feel so passionately about helping others achieve their personal goals in education, in the same way that I have, that I enrolled to complete the PGCE (PCET) programme with Edge Hill University during 2009 after retiring from 30 years police service.

Perhaps one day my mother's dream of my becoming a doctor and mine of being clever, perhaps even being a teacher, will come true. Oz and the Emerald City might be just over the next hill!

Name: Sabeen Hussain
Age: 24
Qualifications: BA (Hons) English Language & Lit.
Specialist Subject: English Language & Literature
Interesting Fact: I was featured on the BBC Talent Writers series, End of Story, which was screened on BBC Three in 2004.

My passion for reading and telling stories came from my love of English Literature. At school I was awarded many prizes and recognised for my flair in creative writing. However, I was born with a complex visual impairment, and I inevitably encountered numerous difficulties when it came to performing the fundamental tasks of reading and writing. These challenges were to increase when at sixteen years old I was diagnosed with Retinitis Pigmentosa, a degenerative eye condition which leads to eventual blindness.

Whilst studying for my GCSEs, I was presented with a formidable challenge which would intensify as time progressed. Whilst studying for my A-Levels at Manchester College for Arts and Technology, the implications of my condition slowly began to emerge and take effect. In spite of this, my fervour for literature was maintained, and I eventually progressed to the University of Manchester to study an undergraduate degree in English Language and Literature.

Despite the stream of obstacles which had arisen over time, I was evermore determined to realise my childhood ambition of becoming a writer. I attained a 2:1 classification in my degree, which demonstrated the possibility that any challenge, regardless of its intensity, could be overcome. I was inspired to pursue a career in teaching in the PCET Sector. During my time at Manchester College of Arts, I had been exposed to the experiences which had proven pivotal to my development. Perhaps one day, these experiences can provide inspiration and motivation for youngsters who I may teach who are suffering similar difficulties as they pursue their own dreams.

It was also during my PCET years that I gained employment as an educational consultant with organisations such as the RNIB and Action for Blind People. I provided specialist staff development training to tutors at both Further and Higher Education Institutions, which helped to raise awareness of the various problems and possible solutions which may arise in the context of teaching and learning for visually impaired students. I was also keen to assist in showing how inclusive practices can be implemented by way of promoting equality of both opportunity and experience.

Since my graduation, I have returned to what has now become The Manchester College, where I am currently training as an English teacher (my own A-Level English teacher being my mentor on this PGCE course). It is a real honour and a privilege to be back amongst many of the individuals who had provided me with the encouragement and support which I needed in order to overcome the obstacles that I faced. It is these very same individuals (and some lovely new faces too) that continue to assist me endlessly and unconditionally.

Whilst training, the fundamental difficulties I experienced, and many more besides, become more apparent. The high level of motivation and positive reinforcement which I aim to instil in my students, together with my enthusiasm for my specialist subject and indeed, teaching, encourage me to continue to fulfil my potential.

Although I have overcome many obstacles since my early adulthood, there are countless more challenges which have yet to come. Hopefully I will qualify as an English teacher though, needless to say, it has already been an incredible journey so far.

I teach... because it is rewarding to develop people's lives and give them the opportunity to do something different. I enjoy meeting new people and this always brings with it new and exciting challenges.

Teaching also allows me to live my own life by giving me a rewarding career with excellent financial opportunities. I am always learning and changing my teaching methods to develop the Learner more.

I hope to be around for many years and take on new and exciting roles.

Lee Innes
Sports Teacher

Name: Fritha Watson
Age: 31
Qualifications: LLB (Hons)
Training to Teach: Law in PCET
Interesting Fact: A great number of my relatives already work in education. I was always adamant that I wouldn't be joining them, but I have now succumbed to my family's calling to educate others!

From the age of fifteen, I was convinced that I was going to be a lawyer. Every choice I made was aimed at achieving that goal. I remember sitting in my first law lecture and knowing that I had made the right choice. Everything I was studying fitted in with who I was and where I wanted my life to go. Then I came to my final year and started applying for training contracts and a place at law school. It was a surprise to realise that my longed for career no longer felt right. There was nothing about the actual job that I still loved; it appeared that all the fun parts had been thrown in the bin, and all the rubbish was left behind.

I was left in a quandary, with no clear idea of what to do; I only knew that I didn't want to be a lawyer. So I studied for a Masters – my love of the law was still there, but only in an academic sense. Whilst completing my dissertation, I started working part-time for a multinational company in their regulatory department. It was law, but it wasn't, and at the time felt like a reasonable compromise. However, I can't claim that it was 'right' – something was still missing. I worked there for over two years, during which time I fell ill.

A nerve in my face was sending pain signals to my brain, even though there was nothing actually wrong. The continual misfires meant that my whole face was left raw and aching, and incredibly sensitive to the slightest thing; a breeze across my face would make me scream.

Although not life-threatening, I was in constant pain and, by the end, was unfit to work due to the pain, the side effects of the drugs I was taking, and a sense of helplessness that I couldn't escape. I was signed off for four years as unfit to work. I could barely leave the house; I only went to see my doctors. They eventually agreed (after about two years) that there was nothing they could do to treat the problem, and I was referred to a pain management clinic so that I could learn to live with the pain. They suggested that I try acupuncture and I found that, for the first time in a long time, I was able to function. It wasn't perfect, and I wasn't 'normal,' but it was an improvement. I was able to think about what I was going to do with the rest of my life.

Throughout my life, I have always fallen into the role of educator without even really realising. At both school and university, my peers would often come to me for clarification on difficult points because they knew that I could explain it so they could understand as well. If someone asked me a question, I couldn't help but give them a complete answer, and prompt them to think about the issue for themselves. So, when the time came for me to seriously consider what I was good at, and what I really wanted to do, I accepted that what I really wanted to do was teach.

Feeling so much better, I enrolled on the City and Guilds 7302 Preparing to Teach course. Everything about it felt right and natural. I completed that course and started the 7407, finding a teaching placement at another college and, finally, moving on with my life.

Then, in the May, I had a sudden and complete relapse. The pain was back, I couldn't go outside anymore, I was unable to complete the course and I sank into a deeper, darker depression than I had ever experienced before. The acupuncture was no longer enough to control the pain. Living with it was the best I could hope for.

The pain levels continued to fluctuate over the next year, rising once more around April/May 2009. By this point I had a new acupuncturist who realised that I always relapsed around the same time each year. She made a connection that no one else had made – that I was always worse in late spring/summer, when the pollen count is high. She theorised that I was allergic to something and my swollen sinuses were compressing the nerve, causing the pain. When I suggested this to my GP, she put me on an antihistamine as an experiment. For the first time in over four years, I had no pain at all. The depression that had dogged me for years lifted – I had found my own personal miracle.

A month later, I was ready to start again. I knew that I wanted to teach, I had already established that it was the right path for me, and having finally found a treatment, I was determined that nothing was going to stop me from following that path and regaining my life. Due to the time of year (it was late June by the time I submitted my application), I went straight through clearing with GTTR, and was offered interviews at both Edge Hill and Newport Universities. I came over to Edge Hill for an Open Day and loved the campus and the staff.

Since starting the course, I have found that, undoubtedly, teaching is the right path for me – everything about it just fits right. I now look forward to the rest of my life, doing something that I love and with a minimum of pain.

Why do I teach? I teach because I love the look on a learner's face when they 'get' something they had previously struggled with. Being part of that process is its own reward.

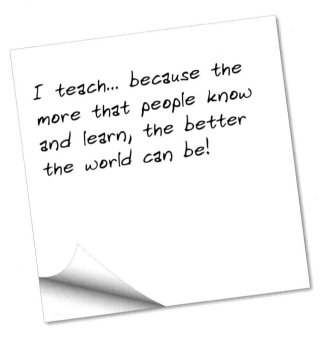

I teach... because the more that people know and learn, the better the world can be!

Jonathan Tummons from Teeside University

Name: Matthew Mugan

Age: 23

Interesting Fact: I knocked my front tooth out running into a wall when I was 8!

Learning journeys aren't like normal journeys. Normal journeys start because you have somewhere to go, and you set off to get there, taking a route you decided on before you left. Then when you arrive, the journey ends.

Learning journeys are different. You set off not knowing where you're going to go, and you have no route planned out, and no maps telling you what roads lead where. But, more importantly, you never end a learning journey. You may arrive at a new place, but only for a moment before you learn something new and the journey continues. I think I realised this fairly early on my journey.

I knew from a very early age that I had set off on the learning journey, the primary school uniform being a big giveaway. Early education is a strange time on a learning journey, because you're not driving your own train (my learning journey is a train, the reasons for which will become more apparent later) and not driving your own train is a very strange thing when you're the only person on board! The pedagogical methods of pre-teen education direct everything you do - you must study this, consider that, paint within the lines. And that was very much how I operated. I did as I was told, stayed on the tracks (see how the train metaphor is coming together) and generally worked through school with good grades.

In high school the process continues, admittedly with less time playing games, but the same theme of being directed through education by someone else.

At the start of my GCSEs when I had to pick my first options, I knew that I was actually the train driver. You have to do the same standard GCSEs but you get to choose 2 from a range of humanities and arts. I chose PE immediately; it was an easy choice. My second choice was trickier. Teachers from all the subject choices tried to attract each student's attention. "Mr. Mugan, you would make an excellent history student," and, "Mugan, have you thought about drama?" I wanted neither and chose art instead. This was my first directional choice in education, and it made me realise that I was starting to drive the train, and I could pick were it was heading.

The end of my journey through high school had ended and my train needed somewhere to go next. I chose the route to college. I wanted to learn more about everything, so I chose Law, Psychology and ICT at A-Level. I drove my train through college for a year, before it became time to think about university. I had always thought I would become a sports student, but I had a hard time settling on it, because there was so much open to me. I looked at everything - nursing, sport, archaeology, business and psychology, but I finally chose architecture. I set the train tracks towards buildings and set off full steam ahead!

Concentrating on my architectural dream by drawing pictures and taking photographs, I failed to pass the exams I needed in order to actually get in. I know what you're thinking - an epic fail right? Well it really wasn't. A learning journey isn't like a normal journey; you don't crash and stop, because even if you're off the rails, you still learn. I got right back on the tracks, and changed direction to keep going.

I pointed the track towards Salford, and particularly towards economics. Why? Because I thought it would be fun. But it wasn't! I spent about 2 months learning economics, before I gave up. But I couldn't leave university; my thirst for learning wouldn't allow me to. I looked at the track that was available to me, and chose a familiar route. The train set off towards sport science central station.

My journeys have always been smooth; I have been well supported by teachers, friends and family. My time as a sport science student was excellent. I couldn't learn enough and, in April 2009, I chose to become a functioning part of the learning process as a career. I chose to teach. I applied for, and was lucky enough to get, a place on the PCET PGCE course at Edge Hill University. Now all I had to do was finish my degree and continue my journey.

I pulled into graduation station in July 2009 and wore the cap and gown for the first time. The sense of achievement was fantastic, but I wanted more and I was happy that I took the choice to continue learning. So now I am journeying through my PGCE, learning so much about teaching as well as learning about myself, my dreams and my aspirations. I love what I do and I love what I know but, most of all, I love what I *will* know. I know my journey will keep on going forever, and I look forward to all the things I will see along the way.

The most important thing I have learned on my journey is this. Good things come to those who wait, but great things wait for no one. You have to go and get what you want in life and learning is how to do this. The journey takes you where you want to go, and you lay the tracks. You drive the train, and visit the places you want to see. But no trains travel when you sit and wait. Trains travel when you don't wait, when you move onwards every day, always wanting to see something new, go somewhere different, and become something better.

Next stop, who knows? All aboard!

I teach... because it means that I can help students to raise their aspirations, change their lives and develop into people who can make a positive difference.

John Bainbridge, Liverpool Community College

Name: Carmel Gibbons
Qualifications: Masters in Education, PGCE, Kew Diploma in Horticulture and BA(Hons) Interdisciplinary Human Studies
Subjects Taught: Horticulture, Numeracy, Sports Turf, Environmental Conservation and Teacher Training
Interesting Fact: I write poetry.

I had attended 5 schools by the time I was 7, due to family breakdown and moving around between England and Ireland. As fast as I learnt things, I lost them and could not write my name when I started the new term at the age of 7. I remember being more shocked than my teachers were, as this was something I was able to do when I was 3 or 4.

Life became more settled for a few years and learning picked up, but when I was 13, my Mum had another breakdown. By the time I was 16, when I was doing my O-Levels, she had started going in and out of hospital on a regular basis and I became a carer for my 13 year old brother. We had to get two buses up to see Mum, but we went every night. My A-Levels were a disaster, as were my brother's O-Levels, but I managed to get into University even though, deep down, I felt like I was stupid. I felt like that all the way through university and though I came out with a 2:2, I couldn't wait to get away from learning. I'd had enough; learning for me had become a strain.

In my mid 20's, I became a gardener and I got a job as an apprentice. I had to attend college on day release, but I suddenly really enjoyed learning and realised that I could learn. It was partly because of the subject, but mainly because learning was linked to my work; something that has stayed with me ever since. I gained my vocational qualifications and worked as a gardener for a few years. I did not think about learning again until I started teaching, when I was expecting my first baby.

I did not do my teacher training immediately but, like a lot of vocational teachers, waited until I got a full-time teaching job. I did my PGCE at Keighley College between my second and third babies. I really enjoyed my PGCE. I had a teacher called John Bewick and he was a huge influence on me. I became fascinated by learning and when I completed my PGCE I started thinking about doing a Masters. I was still plagued with doubts about my academic ability, but was thrilled when I achieved my Masters. Now I had 4 children aged 8, 6, 4 and 2 and was working full-time.

My tutor was very positive about the research that I did for my dissertation and I presented my findings at an academic conference. I thought that perhaps it was a one-off, but I started on the EdD programme. The first year of the EdD is taught and so it gave me the chance to see if I was up to it academically.

I have had to suspend my studies due to changing jobs, but I am determined to complete my research. It is no coincidence that the focus of my research is people who are marginalised within organisations. I think that my Mum's experience, of being marginalised by friends and family as an Irish single parent and, subsequently, as a woman with a mental illness, has had a profound effect on me. I am particularly interested in exploring how organisations could offer support to people in times of crisis. Deep down, I wonder that if my Mum had had the right support when she was going through her crisis, things might have been very different for her.

I teach... because I want people to enjoy learning and to reach their true potential.

I always wanted to learn and to enjoy education but was let down by poor teaching and indifferent teachers.

I am passionate about making sure this does not happen to others.

Jane Wood
Senior Lecturer, Edge Hill University

Name: Craig Gelling
Age: 34
Qualifications: BA (Hons) Literature
Subjects Taught: English, ESOL
Interesting Fact: The first nightclub I managed was destroyed in the largest fire on mainland UK since the Great Fire of London in 1666.

I teach... because I never gave up.

My learning journey is a fractured one, full of wrong turns and dead ends. Before pursuing a career in teaching, I had several other careers; nightclub manager, civil servant, insurance clerk, kitchen porter, door-to-door salesman. None of those jobs offered me the challenge that teaching does. None of those jobs prepared me for the hard work that teaching entails. None of those jobs gave me the reward that teaching does. I chose to follow a career in teaching half-way through my degree in Literature. It was a decision that was a mixture of wanting to feel important, wanting to use the skills I had gained in my previous careers and wanting to indulge my passion for literature.

In June 2006 my life changed. At the time I was thirty years old, had been unemployed for nearly a year and had moved back to Liverpool to live in my mother's house. I felt desolate. All my life I had worked. My last job had been as a manager of a nightclub - a well-paid, responsible position. It had afforded me a decent lifestyle, but ultimately I had been unhappy and wanted something more challenging for my future. After ten months of going to the job centre and signing on, I'd had enough. My mood was as low as it had ever been. I'd withdrawn from my friends, had given up chasing after mediocre jobs and being turned away from training courses because there was no funding. There seemed to be no hope for me. I went to my doctor and told him I was struggling to cope. He told me I was suffering from depression and I couldn't help but agree.

Depression is often misunderstood. There is a stigma attached to it that there isn't to other illnesses. A lot of people seem to assume that suffering from depression is merely a state of mind. They think you should just cheer up and get on with it. They think that you're just being miserable, and that you need to do something to take your mind off it. They think you're weak and useless. They think a lot of things, but they're wrong. Even as I write this, I wonder what people will think of me, knowing that I suffered from depression. But what is more important than people's perceptions and assumptions, is what I think about myself. Ironically, being told I suffered from depression was the catalyst for my life turning around. I wanted to prove to myself that this wasn't going to beat me; that I wasn't going to hide from the challenges that life offered me because of it.

Two months later, I went back to university to study literature. I'd always had a passion for literature and writing. I felt at ease reading and writing and, although the course was difficult, it proved to be just what I needed. I found work while I studied, something I'd been unable to do for over a year. The confidence that learning gave me allowed me to get in touch with friends I'd withdrawn from. The self-esteem I gained from performing well on my course helped me to grow and enjoy life. It was during my second year that I started to think seriously about what I was going to do next. I thought about all of the people that had influenced my life for the better, and each of them had one thing in common. They had educated me, whether academically or otherwise; it was their influence that had helped me to turn things around. I thought back to the time I was unemployed, and wanted to help people like me.

Teaching isn't an easy option. Teaching is hard work, long hours, and a lot of preparation. It takes commitment and sacrifice. Over the last few years, I've had my share of obstacles to overcome. My parents' health, finance, as well as my own condition and barriers to my education remain on the horizon. But in teaching in Further Education, I've seen learners with worse obstacles to overcome. I feel lucky to have the opportunity to participate in educating them, supporting them and hopefully allowing them to achieve their potential, the way others have done for me. I teach because I don't want them to give up. I wouldn't give up this time.

Since that decision, things haven't always gone smoothly. I had to work full-time whilst studying to pay bills; my mother was struck down by illness in the first month of my PGCE and I had to take on the role of carer; and I still have to battle with depression from time to time. But I'm aware that, despite all of this, I'm lucky. I get the opportunity to help people like me to realise their potential. I have trust placed in me on a daily basis that I have learners' best interests at heart. I get to watch people as all of the pieces of the puzzle fit together, like they did for me, and there is no greater reward than that.

I teach... because I want to be a lifelong learner; my students provide me with a variety of experiences that would otherwise be beyond my reach.

Debbie Ralls
Programme leader for teacher education
The Manchester College

Name: Davinder Johal
Occupation: Business Lecturer, Warrington Collegiate Institute
Qualifications: PCET course completed June 2009 - Edge Hill University

My reason for choosing teaching was the fact that I had always thought about it but never been able to pursue it, until now. My family business was feeling the effects of the recession and I had a relevant reason to retrain and quick!

In September 2008, I started the PCET course at Edge Hill and, from the first day, found it a hugely enriching experience. The positive aura I felt there was one of the things that spurred me on.

It was very hectic juggling the assignments with placement training, let alone my 3 demanding children. I made huge sacrifices on a social level as the planning at the start of training takes a long time to master.

I was lucky; my placement mentor was a highly experienced business woman herself, as well as being a high calibre member of staff. At Edge Hill, my tutor was equally experienced in his field and the combination of such expertise made my training all the more valuable and effective.

Towards the end of the course in May, I started looking around for vacancies, but I was surprised at how few were being advertised. I thought it was time to be less formal and start knocking on doors, so I sent an email to the Curriculum Director at Warrington Collegiate Business department. I also sent an up to date CV and a covering letter and literally begged for a job, stating that my business expertise was gained through self-employment in the retail sector.

Following this, I received an email back asking me to come in for a chat, which actually turned out to be an informal interview. Then followed a microteach and the offer of sessional hours from September 2009. Mission accomplished!

My experience in the world of teaching has been both positive and negative. Let's face it, all professions are the same. It is hugely demanding, but I really feel that I have made a difference to the way that students learn, as well as to their confidence. Recently, one of my students secured a part-time job based on the interview skills that I had covered in one of the business units, and his employer commended him on his interview style. My students say that they enjoy my teaching style and that they find my lessons very structured and useful.

Finally, I could say that I teach because the job is ethical, in that you are preparing people for their working life and their success is your reward. I have never before come home from work feeling as fulfilled as I do now - most days!

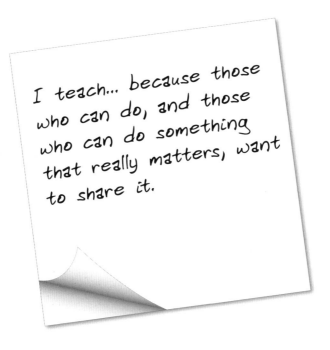

I teach... because those who can do, and those who can do something that really matters, want to share it.

Professor Martin Ashley PhD, MPhil, BEd, FHEA, LTCL
Head of Research (Faculty of Education)
Director, the Centre for Learner Identity Studies

Name: Benjamin Smith

I teach... to inspire, challenge and motivate.

These are just three of the reasons why I have chosen a career in teaching. I am currently a final year undergraduate studying BA (Hons) English Language at Edge Hill University, where I am due to graduate in July 2010.

Shortly before writing this, I read an article in the Daily Mirror about how the gap between the rich and poor is supposedly growing. In the article, there was a commentary on the achievement of white working-class boys in the UK. Although it is true, generally speaking and statistically, that children and young people from poorer backgrounds achieve far less at school than any other demographic group of pupils, I have always believed that young people from tough backgrounds can be aspirational and are able to achieve great things.

As part of my career choice, I have undertaken a lot of voluntary work experience. A great deal of my work has required me to be in classrooms assisting and developing the learning of challenging pupils, something I thoroughly enjoy. It has required energy, commitment, drive and motivation.

I believe that volunteering in schools is a great thing to do. Through my experiences, I have learnt some of the skills that will help me become a better teacher. Pupils might have laughed, sniggered and called me 'mad', but I really believe they respected my efforts to share my skills. In each of the schools I have found placements, I have at some point had the delight of working with groups of challenging pupils. One thing I really encourage is the notion of achievement.

But, of course, when you are dealing with pupils who lack self-belief, getting them to commit to a learning experience can be a tough task. However, I believe in the pupils I see before me. I believe in working with and not against them. They deserve an equal chance to access the help and support they need to make the right choices and achieve their full potential. All of my work is about facilitating pupils to develop their self-belief, offering them greater opportunities and the chance to become better equipped for life's challenges.

I really, really want to make a difference. This is why I want to teach.

I teach... because every learning opportunity opens a door!

Nichola Munro
Associate Lecturer at Edge Hill University

I teach...

I am currently a part-time lecturer in PCET at Ormskirk and at Knowsley Community College, having been a lecturer in the FE sector for nearly 15 years. I taught adults with learning difficulties for about 6 years and then became cross-college coordinator for teacher training courses, and finally the centre programme leader in my former college. I was made redundant by my former college last July but was fortunate enough to secure part-time teaching by September.

Like many people in the Post Compulsory sector, I have had a long and, at times, complex journey. I left school (a single sex grammar school) at 16 with no qualifications, having felt from day one like a very square peg in a very round, Oxbridge-fixated, hole. Parental pressure and the need to find a job to support myself and my daughter sent me scuttling back to Further Education (night classes) to get O-Levels in Maths and English, which enabled me to get a job as a Clerical Assistant with the Ministry of Transport and Environment. I transferred to Manchester from Surrey with my daughter two years later and took up the same post. My managers saw some potential in me and sent me on day release to my local FE College to get additional O-Levels and eventually I was promoted to Clerical Officer.

I gave up work when my daughter was 6 due to her severe health problems. I became a housewife and full-time mum and had another 3 children (all boys, and all born within 5 years). I still went to night classes in my local FE College, to keep my brain ticking over, gaining another O-Level and discovering a love of embroidery, which prompted me to apply to university once my youngest started school.

I loved every second of my Foundation (Art & Design) course. Original plans to do a degree in Embroidery changed very quickly once I had sampled the varied elements of the Foundation course, and by the end of my Foundation year I wanted to apply to do a degree in 3D design. Fortunately, my tutors knew me better than I knew myself and persuaded me to apply to do a degree in Educational Media Design. At last I was a round peg in a round hole and three very happy, very busy years followed. I passed my degree with a 2:1 a few months before my 39th birthday.

I took a year out to concentrate on my children and to decide what to do next. Eventually I was persuaded to try a part-time teacher-training course, at my local college. I wanted to teach in FE because it was only through going to night classes that I had been able to 'start over' in my own education, and I thought I could help other people who had not been successful in their own school lives. I didn't expect to have a career in teaching – I thought I was too old. Fortunately, my new colleagues didn't agree with me and I started paid teaching before I had even finished the first year of my PGCE.

I decided that I wanted to teach adults with learning difficulties, as a way of 'paying my dues'. That sounds a bit pious, but what I mean is that I was one of 8 children, and the mum of 4; my siblings and children are fortunately all healthy and bright and I felt I had a huge debt to repay to FE. Who better to help than those who had not only struggled with school, but who had also struggled with additional difficulties?

In a series of 'happy accidents', my teaching with disadvantaged learners (including youth trainee students and adults returning to learning) and numerous CPD courses, gave me the skills and knowledge I needed to teach a specialist teacher-training course - preparing qualified teachers to teach adults with learning difficulties. Almost before I knew it, I was asked to try teaching on PCET courses and within a year, this became my full-time subject area.

Despite the recent shock of redundancy and the rapid, almost overwhelming changes that have taken place in the PCET sector, I feel privileged to be continuing to teach in this complex and challenging area. I hope some of my experiences will enable students to recognise and appreciate the varied journeys of the learners they will be teaching in the future.

The Lecturer's Lot!

Teacher, counsellor, manager, guide
Administrator (with nowhere to hide)
Devisor of teaching materials and aids
Creative design, is that why we're paid?

Assessment of students (external or not)
Providing tutorial support for the Lot
Creating a perfect environment to learn
It's for all of these things we continue to earn

But the day doesn't stop when the last student leaves
There are still extra-curricular activities
The planning's extensive, where teamwork's a must
And impressive delivery is what earns us a crust

Yet without one thing there's nought to be gained
An evaluation system must be maintained
But prior to this there's a lot to be done
For finding the students is task number one

So marketing skills will also be gauged
In considering the person, the worth and the wage
To select the right people, no more or less
Means we must be adept at the recruitment process

Then once we've assisted in enrolling the mass
A course of inductions tailored for the class
When keeping records of attendance and grades
It's clerical duties for which we are paid

Yet how do we keep up to date with our trade?
Time for our own research has to be made
So if anyone thinks lecturers of today
Only work 9 to 5, they'll be filled with dismay

When you consider the extent of the job
The 'per hour' rate works out at a 'few bob'
That's without all the meetings, committees and groups
Arranging guest speakers and safe field trips

Industrial liaison and lots of PR
It's the widest portfolio I've had by far
In coming to a sensible definition of the role
There aren't enough words to cover the whole

Suffice it to say, having tested my patience
It's not just a job - it's a bloody vocation!

A poem by Peter Kirwin
Travel & Tourism Lecturer, Hopwood Hall College

I teach... because I want children to observe, describe and explain. I don't want them to memorise Newton's laws of motion – I want them to be able to work out for themselves why a skater will crash into the barrier on an ice rink if they don't apply a bit of friction.

One of the most memorable lessons from my career was a very simple one with a fairly difficult class of year 8 pupils. We just had some rocks to look at, and without filling their heads with labels, I asked them to look for words to describe them. By the end of the lesson, they were still enjoying finding new colours and textures.

Matt Cochran
Assistant Head of Secondary Education (Sciences and Mathematics)

Name: Andrew Morris
Age: 42
Qualifications: BA, MA
Subjects Taught: Art and Design
Interesting Fact: I have 11 toes.

I teach... to empower; to pass on what I know.

If I were to believe in social stereotypes, I would assent to the idea that different people have different roles in life, depending on social class, gender and ethnicity.

During my time at primary school, it was the norm to separate pupils into two or three categories, according to higher or lower levels of perceived intelligence understood at that time. Those pupils who passed an exam entered Grammar school; all the rest went either to a tech-school or a secondary modern. It was aimed at engendering roles in society, where the most academically able or the 'top end' went on to enter professional careers such as science, education, medicine, law and the arts. The middle achievers usually went on to do apprenticeships in technical careers such as nursing, clerical or engineering. The 'bottom end' entered the manual labour market to work in factories or other manual areas.

From the age of ten, my cards were marked. I remember the disappointment of not passing my 11 plus and I don't think I ever got over it. It was directed from above that I was to be demoted and become a 'secondary moderner', following my four brothers and sisters who went to the same school.

Having failed to complete a long division sum in the first maths lesson at secondary school, I was demoted again, from the 'top class' in the so-named 'main stream' of education to a remedial programme with all the stigma attached to it. I resigned to my fate as, what was commonly perceived to be, a sub class pupil. I languished there for the next five years where my behaviour got steadily worse as time went on. Truancy and suspensions followed and I left school with three criminal convictions, one qualification and no self-esteem.

I began to wonder whether I was made for the life into which I was born. What to do? Where to go to get out of this mess I found myself in? The mother's wing of the armed forces seemed like a good way out. They take on all kinds of waifs and strays, regardless of education, so one year after I left school, I embarked upon a career in the army.

Three years later, I had gathered myself again and instilled enough discipline and self-respect to start to think about what I was going to do next. I began to think what my strengths were and concluded that the arts were the right place for me. With one year to go in the army, I had secured a place on a visual arts foundation course on the strength of a portfolio of art work. During this final year in the army, I decided to prepare for college by taking an Open University course on 16th Century Italian Renaissance Art. Eight months before I was to leave the army, I was informed that I would be called for duty in what was to be the first Gulf war. This is what I would call 'a minor setback' to my studies and to my future plans, post-army. War or no war, enemy or no enemy, desert or no desert, I *was* going to finish my OU assignments, and so I did, sand and all.

From the foundation course, I gained a place on a degree programme, followed by a Masters Degree programme the following year. Since that time I have lived, worked and enjoyed a career as an artist in London, USA, India and Bulgaria.

Amongst many other reasons, the arrival of a baby allowed me to revaluate my priorities, so after three years in the wilderness of Bulgaria, my family and I returned to the UK. I had already made plans to re-enter education, only this time the idea was to become a teacher. I did some research to find the most effective route into teaching within further and higher education. I found the best course to do and here I am.

I teach... because I want to inspire, aspire, empower and open doors to new opportunities!

Rohema Khan
Associate Lecturer at Edge Hill University

Name: Norma Kelly
Age: 54
Qualifications: Diploma in Management, HNC Business & Management (CertEd pending!)
Subjects Taught: Business, Japanese Business Management (Kaizen), Project Management, Effective Listening, Team Building, Employability Skills

'A star always shines'
Those inspirational words were said to me by a tutor when completing my HNC. I was forty years of age. Eleven years later I started to teach.

The eldest of four children, I left school at 16 to work as a typist. College and further education were out of the question as our family needed the extra income. Money was tight in 1972. So although an excellent student who loved school, and whose head was always buried in a book, I flunked exams as I couldn't see the point...
why try when I had to work?

After 25 years working, I was frustrated at being told to keep my opinions to myself as I was only 'the typist'...
what did I know?

I knew that I taught each newcomer how to use office equipment and IT, how to answer the phone and communicate with different levels of management and the public, how to relate office protocol and legislation to their role, how to support colleagues, and much much more...
but were my efforts so insignificant?

All it took was one person to acknowledge those efforts to once more ignite the passion to learn that had been lost for so many years...
they believed in me!

This spark rekindled a yearning to be the best I can be. Embracing new opportunities was the catalyst to moving out of my comfort zone into scary and unknown areas...
my life changed dramatically!

Challenging, hard work, at times frustrating, but always enlightening and rewarding, three years later I manage multi-million pound ICT projects. Always learning from people, always teaching others along the way; I retired at the age of 50, happy and content...
so what next?

The common thread throughout my life was teaching someone to do something, but I hadn't realised it until now. Teaching my brother to ride his bike, my sisters how to bake, a friend how to swim, a colleague how to cope; in return they all taught me more than I could ever learn from just books, and for that I thank them. People always said I would make a good teacher but I never believed them, because then I didn't believe in myself...
now I do – all it took was someone to tell me!

This learning journey is something we all embark on from the day we are born and I believe that learning from others has brought me to this realisation today...
why teach?

I teach... because I want to learn
I teach... because I believe in you

The reason I teach can't be summed up in a single sentence. I'm passionate about my subject, sure, but I could have indulged that passion in other ways. The main reason I teach is because it makes a difference.

The other day, a student ran after me to tell me she'd just been accepted at uni to do a degree in psychology, and thanked me for helping her switch on to the subject. And during the Easter break, some of my students came in to work on their assignments when they could have been at home eating chocolate eggs!

It can be hard work but, ultimately, it's incredibly rewarding.

Angela Court-Jackson
Lecturer in Health Care and Education, Southport College

Name: Saqib Hussain
Subject Taught: Numeracy, Maths to adult learners
Qualifications: ACA, BA (Hons)
Interesting Fact: I am a published poet.

I worked as an auditor/accountant for a few years after university and, although I learnt a lot, I never really enjoyed the work and found there was very little appreciation. The hours were often long, including weekend work, and I felt I was just churning out accounts and audit working papers, without making much visible difference.

I had considered teaching since university and, when made redundant by my employer, I felt it was time to take the risk. It was an unknown field but it was either that, or spend the rest of my life thinking 'what if'.

I have always enjoyed giving advice and helping others, without expecting anything in return – teaching offered a perfect platform for this with the added bonus of more job satisfaction. Although my family were cautious at first, they came round to the idea, hoping it would be something I would find more rewarding and manageable.

I wanted to focus more on teaching than discipline and felt students in FE would be more committed and motivated, so there should be fewer discipline problems – although I understand this is not the case everywhere. Thankfully my classes, on the whole, have been well behaved allowing me to focus on teaching.

I had to consider finances knowing I would be earning less than I had been used to, but I saw the benefits as far outweighing the costs, including greater wellbeing.

An interesting fact about me is I write poetry – I have had a few poems published and have written one on my experience so far:

Working frantically in an office
Staring at a computer all day
This deadline, that deadline, never stops
Should I leave, or should I stay?

If I stay I will always wonder
Whether things can be better elsewhere
Better to dive in, take a risk
Life's too short to be running scared

Teaching is interesting in that
You give, but get out much more
And I can't help but notice that
The acts of teaching, and learning, are in our core

Since the beginning of time people taught
And people learnt, and we all grew
Let knowledge be spread, and used, by the masses
Not restricted to a self-selected few

And bring positivity to each interaction
And each interaction gladly cherish
Give, because truly "to give is to live
And to withhold is to perish".

by Saqib Hussain

I teach... because no matter how hard it can get or how much marking I have to do, every now and then I have a 'light bulb moment' with a student and they understand what it is that I've been waffling on about.

Arnie Breen
Performing Arts Lecturer (Acting)
Brooksby Melton College

Name: Catherine Shiel
Age: 37
Qualifications: English Degree
Subjects Taught: Business

I teach... to help people to grow in their confidence and grow in their potential.

Why do you want to be a teacher? You must be insane! Isn't the pay rubbish?

I can just see you doing that! I would have stayed in education if I'd had a teacher like you!

These are the opposing ends of the scale of comments I received, and still do, when I tell people I have made the decision to go into teaching.

I was a manager in the retail sector, working for a large national company. Operational pressures and the need to deliver great performances were central to my role. However, I always found time and energy to invest in my team. It mattered to me, and I often found the reward from that far outweighed being top on a performance leader board. As a result, I veered towards a career in Learning & Development which became my passion. I felt I had found a role I was born to do. I was highly engaged in my job and was recognised and rewarded for my hard work and success. I was at the top of my career and nearing 40, so why change?

My son was born in 2006 and I returned to full-time work after 10 months. For the first time I began to question what I was doing and didn't feel satisfied. At first I blamed this change in outlook on my emotions, going back to work after having a baby is a big thing; so everyone kept telling me. I simply wasn't happy. I felt under pressure to prove I could still do the job. Of course I could still do it, and juggle a family and home life to boot!

And that's what I did. But I began to resent the constant compromises being a career mother presents. When I was working, I felt I was neglecting my husband and son as well as family and friends. At work, I always felt there was more I needed to do to match the level I had worked to previously. I also felt the need to match others around me who didn't have the same commitments and responsibilities and were prepared to make work their first priority, as I once did. There was also the fact that the higher up the ladder I had got, the less training and development I was doing. I was now a game player in a battle of business politics and hidden agendas. I couldn't be further away from what I loved most, which was developing people.

What did I do about it? I did nothing! I was the main bread winner and provided financial security for my family. People depended on me. I just couldn't bring myself to complain, to tell people I wasn't happy. I had the status, the car, the money, a great husband and gorgeous baby boy. What did I have to complain about?

For 18 months I did nothing. I hid away in the comfort of what I knew, collected the pay each month and kept my head down. It was exhausting trying to motivate myself at work.

I am a believer that things happen for a reason and, in 2009, I had the opportunity to take redundancy. Rather than see this as the end of the road, I saw an exciting crossroads of new opportunities. I opened up to my husband and friends and told them how I had been feeling.

I began to explore what to do next. I knew I wanted to find another career - with 10 to 15 years ahead of me, why not? I wanted to find something satisfying that would get me back to developing people. I did my degree 18 years ago with teaching in mind, but at that time in my life it wasn't right for me; maybe now it was.

To retrain meant a financial sacrifice, and I debated over it for several months. Although we feel the pinch and will do for a few years yet, I just think ahead and know it won't be forever. The money, the status, the perks and the BMW have all gone - but I am happy and excited about my new career. Hard work, focus and commitment are still required. However, the rewards are greater. I am challenged and inspired every day by students with more honesty and insight than many of the people I met in the corporate world. I enjoy daily debates and discussions with like-minded people who genuinely share my passion for learning. With good planning and organisation, I can enjoy a work-life balance that gives me quality time with my husband, little boy, family and friends. I feel proud to say what I do and I am proud of the choice I made.

I chose teaching in the Lifelong Learning Sector, because I want to encourage and help people to take responsibility for their own development and their future. There were distinct moments in my life where a teacher (not the college) and managers (not the company) helped me to take charge of my development. They played their part in opening new doors and horizons I had not thought possible for someone from my background. I will always remember them. If I too can play my part in helping someone to do the same, then that will be the most valuable reward and recognition I could hope to achieve.

I teach... because to help facilitate an individual's learning journey is a true privilege. I have learnt so much from an incredibly rich and diverse array of students, as we have shared our teaching and learning experiences together.

Steve Ingle
Senior Lecturer in Post-Compulsory Education and Training
Edge Hill University

Name: Peter Raftery
Age: 49
Qualifications: ACMA
Subjects Taught: Accounting, Numeracy, Finance, Management, Business
Interesting Fact: My son and I play chess by email as a way of keeping in touch while he's studying in London.

I teach... because I want to help others to realise and achieve their potential.

Fourteen years ago, we moved as a family of three up to St Helens, Merseyside. I didn't particularly want to leave Bristol but my other half had been promoted and we had moved so much, following jobs all over the country.

Work for me was scarce, so we decided that I would stay at home for a while and be there for our son as he'd had four different schools in three years, and that's a lot of change for a six year old. After two weeks, I got a bit bored and went to the local College and signed up for a GCSE in Accounting and a Clait course as I didn't know how to switch on a computer! I was hooked. The GCSE became an A-Level and then a professional accountancy qualification with CIMA, the Chartered Institute of Management Accountants.

It was hard to break into the finance work world, but I persevered and my first finance job at the age of 36 was colouring clock cards in a Payroll Department for a huge logistics company. But I kept my ears and eyes open and one job led to another. Meanwhile, I was studying at night and weekends.

During this time, I became a single parent and my son and I muddled along. It was very hard at times but I had a goal – I was going to be a qualified accountant - and that vision kept me moving forward. After a long hard slog, I got there. I had qualified and was able to put the initials ACMA after my name. I was so proud of myself because it's not easy juggling work, family life and studying.

I was promoted and became a Finance Manager, but I started having problems with my hip and ended up on two crutches with severe osteoarthritis, barely able to get in and out of the car, but too young for a hip replacement. The pain was horrendous, but eventually I found a surgeon who agreed to give me a hip replacement.

During my time off work after the surgery, I took time out to look at my life and what I really wanted to do. Sometimes, when something major has happened, it makes you stop and think. I wasn't enjoying the job that I was in, driving 60 miles round trip with too much management and not enough accounting. I needed a more active job closer to home. So I asked myself a lot of questions and I looked back over the different jobs I'd done and thought about what I had really enjoyed about them.

The answer dawned on me. What I had really enjoyed was the teaching, training, coaching and mentoring aspects of the jobs I had done. Sitting alongside someone and helping them understand how to read the monthly statements; explaining how double entry worked and watching their face light up as the penny dropped; doing someone's appraisal and encouraging them to see their potential and give them some help and direction; showing a colleague how to make a spreadsheet more user-friendly. This is what I had enjoyed – I wanted to be a teacher and here I am.

Name: Danielle Vipond
Age: 30
Qualifications: BSC Leisure Management, MA Marketing , studying for a PGCE in PCET
Subjects Taught: Business, Travel & Tourism and Work Skills
Interesting Fact: I play Sunday league football.

I teach... because I want to pass on the knowledge that I have learned and hopefully be an inspiration to someone.

I was the first one of my family to go to university and I spent six years after finishing my Masters whilst working in marketing at a law firm in Manchester. I was diagnosed with dyslexia when I was in sixth form, but it did not stop me from getting a degree in Leisure Management and a Masters in Marketing.

In May 2009, I was made redundant and the world that I was used to came tumbling down. I spent months looking for work with no luck. I had to really think about my future. Throughout the past year, I had seen teaching adverts. I had looked into courses that I could do whilst working, as I could not justify giving up work to follow my dream. After finishing my Masters, I had considered going into teaching, but my confidence was too low to stand in front of a class. I feel I am very lucky as my family, especially my husband, have been very supportive.

Once I had sorted out the financial side of changing my career, I felt a lot more comfortable with my choice. I wanted to teach young people and adults, and wanted to teach something I was interested in and passionate about. I feel this is what makes a good teacher. I loved the marketing element in my management degree, which is why I continued on to do my Masters in the subject. I also enjoyed the six years that I worked in the marketing industry and I hope that this will show in my teaching.

Looking back over the past year, even though I probably went through the worst experience in my life, it has opened up the opportunity for the best career move I have ever made. The course and teaching is very intense, but I love every minute of it.

I teach... because I get great pleasure from being a part of the process where an individual is offered guidance and support in order to realise their own potential and worth within a learning context.

Margaret Postance
Head of Post Compulsory Education & Training
Faculty of Education, Edge Hill University

Name: Lorraine Compton
Age: 23
Qualifications: BA (Hons) History with Dance
Subjects Taught: History and Politics
Interesting Fact: I am only 5ft tall, but try to make up for it in personality!

I teach... because it is my passion and I want to share it with everyone!

I am 23 and this is my first career. I grew up in Devon, and feel very lucky to have done so, as every day I got to experience the beautiful green surroundings of my home village. The reason I chose teaching is because I love interacting with people, meeting new people and learning about people's histories. I have always been interested in what makes people who they are, and I think that a key link in that development journey is their time at school and college.

I definitely believe in the power of education to change someone's life for the better. I know this may seem a little grand, but an amazing number of people walk around with their eyes to the ground, not thinking about these things and therefore not trying to do anything about them.

My main inspiration in all aspects of my life comes from my beautiful family. My family have supported me immensely, and inspire me every day to achieve my maximum potential in whatever I choose. I chose academia, but they would have supported me just as much had I chosen to leave school at 16 and go into work.

I enjoyed school and, in college, I had a wonderful history teacher who encouraged me every day. I also had something to prove as some in my family were not able to go to college due to financial constraints or a lack of, or missed, opportunity.

I still faced several obstacles to achieving my goals, despite the support I received at home. These obstacles came in the form of learning difficulties. Whilst studying at A2-Level, my history teacher felt that I was dyslexic and set the ball rolling for me to receive that little extra help, which ultimately turned my grades around. Without her help, and then that of the many learning support members I have worked with, I would probably still be fighting to get here!

The other obstacle was one of self-confidence. Like many teenagers at school my confidence suffered, particularly due to the school yard bullying I had to face on a daily basis. It was never much more than singling me out so that people would notice certain things about me, but that was enough to make me want to just disappear. I am sure that it affected my engagement at school but, with the help of my friends and my family, I was able to overcome it. I made the decision to go to a college out of my area, which turned out to be one of the best decisions I ever made! I met new people, experienced new subjects and got my confidence back!

I think stories like this are really important, and something to be encouraged. Providing people have the motivation and the support behind them, they can achieve their potential and reach their goals a thousand times over!

One of the joys of working as an academic in research on higher education is the variation in settings, disciplines and most of all the people who I meet and work with from hour to hour.

One morning I will be in a theatre talking to undergraduates who study Dance and by the afternoon I find myself in a cafe with mature students who are learning to be teachers at FE colleges.

Dr. Frances Tracy, Cambridge University

A Note on Reflection

Keeping reflective journals and engaging in critical reflection is a core element of your teacher training. It involves reflecting on your own development needs, your practice and the impact on your students and their learning.

In the beginning, it is difficult to grasp and to engage in reflection in a meaningful way. The word is used constantly, and yet it is difficult to explain or have explained. Through practice, it soon becomes habit forming and then you will find you can't stop reflecting - on everything you do! Getting to this point is a valuable experience, and one that enriches your professional development and practice, and potentially your personal life.

We won't attempt to explain reflection. Instead we provide examples from Amy, who shares her reflections during her teacher training. We hope you gain a sense of reflection, what it is and its value during your journey into teaching.

Looking back on something that didn't go so well and how that felt:

"I felt nervous, as this was my first session teaching, as well as my first observed session. Using an icebreaker to get to know the students a little better relaxed me. I panicked when I was unable to answer a question, when in any other situation I would honestly say I didn't know. This made me feel a little idiotic, but I did manage to move on with some assistance. I didn't deal with the disengaged student effectively and I am kicking myself for this, I need more skills to be able to engage students. Otherwise I enjoyed the lesson and feedback from students was positive."

Looking back on what did go well and why it went well:

"I was very relaxed during the session, which was quite surprising, but I think this was due to being so well prepared."

"All students were engaged in activity and using groups led to much more effective responses, Petty (2009) discusses how groups can do things together that learners cannot do on their own."

Catherine Shiel and Amy Johnson

I teach... because I was lucky enough to be taught by individuals who inspired me to make several choices in my working life, which all turned out to be for the best. Now I am the teacher and I, too, believe that I can help to change other people's lives.

Angela Brzeski
Associate Tutor, Edge Hill University

Reaching Out to Communities

Inclusion and involvement are popular words in further and higher education – but in teacher training we still have some progress to make if we are to reach out successfully to all sections of our society. Despite determined efforts to widen participation at all levels, it is clear that we can do better when it comes to attracting non-traditional and black or minority ethnic groups into Post Compulsory Education and Training and, here at Edge Hill, that's what we strive to do.

So what do we need to address? A recent taster session held in Oldham demonstrated very clearly that we can sometimes be the architects of our own troubles. When it comes to the application process, for instance, it appears we are simply not speaking the same language! Academics (like industrialists, financiers and PR people) love acronyms, but sometimes we forget that what is everyday jargon to us means absolutely nothing to those outside our sphere.

Experience shows us that potential recruits, particularly those from non-traditional sectors, can be put off by the minefield that is the application process, and whether it is the over-enthusiastic use of capital letters or a heavy reliance on the internet and form filling, our approach can quickly alienate some of the people we would love to attract. Geographic location can be a problem too, as can a perceived lack of flexibility when it comes to training routes, especially for more mature candidates.

It's obvious really. A woman from an ethnic minority group, out of the mainstream workforce for 15 years bringing up a family, is probably not going to stroll into a university or college to ask for an application form.

A white working class man recently made redundant and looking for a new challenge is unlikely to turn his attention to teaching, thinking that academic life can offer nothing to him in middle age and with 'outdated' qualifications.

A woman with ongoing responsibility for older parents may write off teaching because she thinks the demands of training can't possibly fit around her family commitments.

Wrong, wrong and wrong! Teaching in schools or in further education can be an option for all those people and we have made huge strides in recognising that harnessing this potential pool of talent requires a different approach. By thinking carefully about venues, flexible course structure and even catering arrangements, we can overcome some of the barriers to recruitment.

In running a recent taster session aimed at minority groups, we learned a lot about what works and what doesn't. By basing ourselves in the community, we instantly became more accessible and less intimidating. By teaming up with specialists who have close links with the town's minority groups, we improved our own local knowledge. Being with potential recruits for three full days really helped us understand what it's like to be 'on the outside, looking in' and made us see how we can make changes that will make a difference.

Of course, attracting applications from minority groups is not a new problem. We know from a 2005 review of Further Education colleges that the workforce lacks diversity. It is estimated that only 6% of FE staff come from minority groups compared to 14% of students.

Minority groups of all types are under represented in teaching, but wouldn't it be good to close the gap and have a workforce which more closely mirrors 21st century society structure? Perhaps an influx of teachers with working class roots, who know the heart of the community could help address the barriers which include lack of social capital that some children from working class backgrounds face. Many don't have parents who can navigate them through the complex system of higher education; it remains cloaked in mystery – unreachable, unimaginable! The emergence of more role models from all marginalised groups would surely be a good thing, not only for education but society. Recognising the structural inequalities such as class, gender and ethnicity is vital to this. In an age of globalisation and competitive markets, many people who fall behind blame themselves – neoliberalism and individualism encourage this. They get the knocks, society's inequalities continue.

We have to remain determined to reach across the boundaries, build communities where people work together, not alone to build their own empires whilst others are left behind. Community and working together in a more egalitarian approach is something Edge Hill University has been committed to for some time, and we won't rest on our laurels.

Cultural, religious and language differences can either be barriers or can be elements which enrich all our lives. If turning a barrier into a benefit just needs a little more outreach - and a lot less jargon - it has got to be worth the effort!

Vicky Duckworth
Senior Lecturer & Course Leader for Full-time PCET
Edge Hill University

I teach... because it has become so much a part of who I am that I cannot conceive of a better profession to be part of. Watching new teachers experience the 'glow' that comes from putting what I have taught them into practice in their own classrooms makes the exhaustion, the juggling of priorities and the occasionally tedious aspects of the job pale into insignificance.

It is quite simply the best game in town.

Lindsey Marsh
Associate Lecturer at Edge Hill University

How to Apply for Teacher Training

Undergraduate Training Courses:
Apply to UCAS - the organisation responsible for managing applications to higher education courses in the UK. Courses leading to QTS have course codes beginning with an X. You can find these by searching for QTS in the course search. There will be a range of universities that you could apply to and you should acquire further information from their websites and if possible visit the universities you are interested in e.g. by attending open events.

Postgraduate Training Course:
If you already have a degree, you can train to be a teacher by either completing a PGCE – Postgraduate Certificate in Education or by SCITT - School Centred Initial Teacher Training. Apply via the GTTR – Graduate Teacher Training Registry – for both of these routes. For the post compulsory sector you should also visit the Lifelong Learning UK website for providers who are not using the GTTR. This will give you details of all full-time and part-time routes and how to apply – usually to individual universities and colleges.

When to Apply:
It is important to do your research as early as possible for all routes into teaching. You need to make sure that you have the necessary qualifications and experience for entry so that you match the selection criteria. Early September is the best time to apply for both undergraduate and postgraduate courses. At Edge Hill University the Careers Centre encourages all students who want to apply for PGCEs to do so by the end of September as the most popular PGCE programmes may be full by Christmas.

Teach First:
Apply via the Teach First website at http://graduates.teachfirst.org.uk/index.html

Graduate Teacher Programme:

For this employment based route respond to an advertisement or find a school prepared to employ and support you through the training process. You can also apply to an Employment Based Initial Teacher Training (EBITT) provider. Details of these are on the TDA website and you can contact those in your region for their specific recruitment details.

Career Prospects:

There are a number of ways in which teachers can progress in their careers, either within the classroom or in a leadership role. You could become curriculum manager, head of a department or key stage co-ordinator or have responsibility for a specific area such as special educational needs or pastoral care. Ultimately you could progress to a senior management level position such as a head teacher.

Help with Getting your First Teaching Post:

Your university careers service and tutors should help you with this. At Edge Hill University the Careers Centre and Faculty of Education work closely in partnership to prepare initial teacher trainees for applying for their first teaching post. This includes a very practical range of website links and information, specific inputs into the curriculum on job applications and interviews, guest speakers and a nationally recognised Teachers Fair with employers attending from all over the country.

Jacqui Howe

Useful Websites

- www.tda.gov.uk – provides comprehensive information on all forms of teacher training including undergraduate & postgraduate training and employment based routes such as the Graduate Teaching Programme and Teach First. Also there are tips on applying, skills tests, and the latest up to date information in the sector. There is also information on how to get work experience

Undergraduate Training
- www.ucas.com – to apply for undergraduate programmes, with details of all courses available

Postgraduate Training
- www.gttr.ac.uk – to apply for postgraduate provision with information on all PGCEs available, including some post-compulsory

Post Compulsory (further education) Training
- www.lluk.org – for information on training as a teacher in the post compulsory sector

Other
- www.gtce.org.uk – General Teaching Council for England
- http://curriculum.qcda.gov.uk – National Curriculum
- www.standards.dfes.gov.uk/ - The Standards website
- www.dcsf.gov.uk - UK government department with responsibility for children's services, families, schools, 14-19 education, and the Respect Taskforce
- http://www.prospects.ac.uk – graduate careers website containing useful information on the sector

Routes into Teaching

Level	Undergraduate	Postgraduate	E
Description	Train to teach whilst completing a degree (3-4 years)	Train to teach if you already have a degree (1-2 years)	Train and (school or (Lifelong Le
	⬇	⬇	
Qualification	BEd Degree BA/BSc with QTS	Postgraduate Certificate in Education (PGCE) School Centred Initial Teacher Training (SCITT)	• Graduate • Registere • Teach Fir • Preparin Learning S • Certifica Learning S • Diploma Learning S
Edge Hill offers:	BA QTS programmes in: • Primary • Keystage 2/3 • Secondary • Post Compulsory Education & Training (PCET / Lifelong Learning))	PGCE Programmes in: • Primary • Secondary • PCET / Lifelong Learning	In-service / Lifelong I PTLLS thro

ment-based aining	Assessment-based training	Overseas trained teacher
hilst working in a r other part of the ector	If you have substantial teaching experience but do not have QTS / QTLS	If you have qualified as a teacher in another country
↓	↓	↓
r Programme (GTP) er Programme (RTP) ch in the Lifelong (LLS) ching in the Lifelong (LLS) ing in the Lifelong (LLS)	• Assessment-based Training Programme	• Overseas Trained Teacher Programme
for teachers in the PCET Sector – DTLLS, CTLLS, Cert. HE / PGCE routes		

Further information on all of these programmes is available at www.tda.gov.uk
To see Edge Hill specific courses, please visit www.edgehill.ac.uk

Afterword

The reasons why people choose teaching vary from person to person. Each route is different and the barriers, challenges and joys encountered along the way are all very different.

The editors of this book met whilst trainees on the PCET PGCE Course at Edge Hill University, under the supervision of Senior Lecturer and Course Leader, Vicky Duckworth. We found the different experiences of our fellow trainees fascinating and a source of inspiration. Sharing stories and journeys travelled has been an enriching experience. In pulling together this book, one thing is clear - that if you are committed to teaching as a career, there are routes available to you, no matter what the barriers.

We share these journeys with you in the hope that you too will find inspiration, encouragement or simply feel empowered to start your journey into teaching. There are many careers guides, websites and university pages on how to become a teacher but, sometimes, hearing someone else's story will have the biggest impact. It did for us!

Editorial Team:
Vicky Duckworth, Craig Gelling, Catherine Shiel and Bernard Sheridan